Garter Snakes

BY ELIZABETH RAUM

amicus
high interest

Amicus High Interest is an imprint of Amicus
P.O. Box 1329, Mankato, MN 56002
www.amicuspublishing.us

Library of Congress Cataloging-in-Publication Data
Raum, Elizabeth.
 Garter snakes / by Elizabeth Raum.
    pages cm. -- (Snakes)
Includes index.
 Summary: "Explains garter snakes including what they eat,
where they live, and information about their life cycle and
interaction with humans"--Provided by publisher.
 Audience: K to Grade 3.
 ISBN 978-1-60753-374-0 (library binding) -- ISBN 978-1-
60753-422-8 (ebook)
 1. Garter snakes--Juvenile literature. I. Title.
 QL666.O636R38 2014
 597.96'2--dc23
                                        2012036390

Editor   Wendy Dieker
Series Designer   Kathleen Petelinsek
Page production   Red Line Editorial, Inc.

Photo Credits
Lyle E. Doberstein/Shutterstock Images, cover; Richard
Nelson/123RF, 4; Chris Hill/123RF, 7; Evan Yokum/123RF, 8;
Steve Byland/Dreamstime, 11; Jason Ross/123RF, 12; Bruce
MacQueen/123RF, 14; iStockphoto/Thinkstock, 17; Lorraine
Swanson/Dreamstime, 18; Matt Jeppson/Shutterstock
Images, 21; 123RF, 22; Jason Mintzer/Shutterstock Images,
25; Tom Brakefield/Stockbyte/Thinkstock, 26; Teresa
Gueck/123RF, 29

Printed in the United States at Corporate Graphics in North
Mankato, Minnesota
4-2013/1149
10 9 8 7 6 5 4 3 2 1

Table of Contents

Fast Snakes

Garter snakes are fast. They dart across the road into the long grass. They lay on a brick wall soaking up the sun. Walk closer, and the snake races away. A flash of wiggly snake catches us by surprise.

Garter snakes slither quickly.

You may find garter snakes in your gardens. Some people even call garter snakes "garden snakes." *Garter snake* is the right name. Garter snakes live in fields, forests, and swamps. They are one of the most common snakes in North America. Garter snakes probably live near you.

 Are garter snakes dangerous?

A garter snake pokes its head through some leaves.

 Not at all. Garters are harmless.

This garter has yellow
stripes from head to tail.

 Q Do snakes feel slimy?

There are many different kinds of garter snakes. Garters are thin. Most are about 28 inches (71 cm) long. Garters may be dark brown, olive green, or red. Some have checks or patterns on their bodies. They all have three long, narrow stripes on their backs. The stripes can be yellow, white, blue, or green.

 No. Their scales are rough and dry.

Catching Lunch

Garters hunt during the day. They have good eyesight and a strong sense of smell. Garters smell with their tongues. They flick their tongues out to collect scents in the air. An organ in the snake's mouth tells the snake what it smells. Is it another garter or something to eat?

Garters flick their tongues to smell the air.

Garter snakes capture their **prey** and swallow it live. They use their teeth and throat muscles to pull prey into their stomachs. Garters eat worms, slugs, and grasshoppers. They also eat bird eggs and mice. Near ponds, they munch on frogs and tadpoles.

This garter snake is looking for something to eat.

Garter snakes lie in the
sun to stay warm.

 **Q** What happens if a garter snake gets too cold?

Seeking the Sun

Garters need the sun. After eating, they **bask**, or lie in the sun. The sun helps them to **digest** their food. Garters need the sun to stay warm, too. Like all snakes, garter snakes are **cold-blooded**. Their bodies cool down when the weather does.

The snake begins to move more slowly. If it doesn't warm up quickly, its heart will stop. It will die.

When the weather gets cool, garters find warm shelters. Some burrow under dead leaves. In colder places, they dig holes underground. It is warmer there. They may crawl into some other animal's den. Garters' bodies slow down. They **hibernate**, or sleep, until spring.

Garters find a den to sleep in all winter.

Red-sided garter snakes live in Canada. They are the only snakes that live that far north. It gets cold there. In winter, these garters crawl into caves deep underground. As many as 20,000 garters might live together in one cave. They stay underground for about six months.

Many garter snakes come out of caves in spring.

Spring Surprise

Garters everywhere wake up in the spring. A woman in Utah met a garter close-up one spring day. She was baking bread. She left the oven door open to cool. When she went to close the door, she peeked inside. She came face-to-face with a 16-inch (40 cm) garter snake. It wanted a warm place to stay.

In the spring, garters look
for places to warm up.

Males and females come together to mate.

 **Q** How do the males smell the females?

In the spring, garters may come inside houses or bask on sunny playgrounds. They are trying to get warm. They **mate** in the spring, too. Females give off a special smell. Many males may gather around one female and form a mating ball. They make a pile of wriggling snakes.

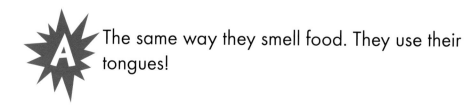

The same way they smell food. They use their tongues!

After mating, ten to 40 babies grow inside the mother's body. Two or three months later, the babies are born live. Baby garters are 4 to 9 inches (10 to 23 cm) long. They already know how to hunt. A few hours after birth, they leave their mother and go hunting. Young garters eat a lot. They must grow before winter comes.

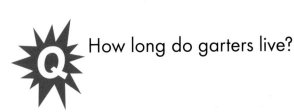
How long do garters live?

This young garter already knows how to hunt.

 Many die in the first year. Most garter snakes live only 2 years.

A hawk catches a garter snake for a meal.

 Is a garter snake's bite deadly?

Lots of Garters

There are lots of garter snakes in North America. They eat many animals that are pests. They eat insects, mice, snails, and slugs. Bigger animals hunt garter snakes. Hawks, raccoons, bigger snakes, and bullfrogs hunt garters. If garter snakes are attacked, they bite and give off a bad smell.

 No. But it hurts. The smell is just stinky.

Next time you see a garter snake, don't be afraid. Garters are harmless. In fact, they help us by eating bugs and other pests. Look closely at the colors. Watch the way the snake winds across the grass. It's fun to watch as the garter slithers away.

Keep an eye out for garters darting in the grass!

Glossary

bask To lie in the sun.

cold-blooded To have the same temperature as the outside air or environment.

digest To turn food into energy.

hibernate To sleep through the winter in a warm place.

mate To come together to create young.

prey An animal that is hunted for food.

Read More

Osborne, Mary Pope and Natalie Pope Boyce. *Snakes and Other Reptiles*. New York: Random House. 2011.

Stewart, Melissa. *Snakes*. Washington, D.C. : National Geographic Society, 2009.

Wallach, V. *Garter Snakes*. Mankato, Minn.: Capstone Press, 2009.

Websites

Eastern Garter Snake Page
http://www.neoperceptions.com/snakesandfrogs.com/scra/snakes/garter.htm

Garter Snakes
http://www3.northern.edu/natsource/REPTILES/Garter1.htm

San Diego Zoo Animal Bytes: Snakes
http://www.sandiegozoo.org/animalbytes/t-snake.html

Index

About the Author

Elizabeth Raum has worked as a teacher, librarian, and writer. She has written dozens of books for young readers. She really enjoyed learning more about snakes. "Snakes are amazing," she says. "But I wouldn't want one for a pet." Visit her website at http://www. elizabethraum.net.